VOLUME 2

SONGS FROM THE HEART

First published in Great Britain in 2018

British Library Cataloguing in Publication Data

A record for this book is available from the British Library

ISBN: 978-1-912373-41-3
Designed by Diane Warnes
Printed in the UK

10Publishing, a division of 10ofthose.com
Unit C, Tomlinson Road, Leyland, PR25 2DY, England
Email: info@10ofthose.com
Website: www.10ofthose.com

Graham Hooper

48 UNDATED DEVOTIONS THROUGH PSALMS 51–100

INTRODUCTION

Structure

The book of psalms is a collection of 150 psalms (songs and poems), divided up into five smaller 'books' as follows:

- Book 1: Psalms 1–41;
- Book 2: Psalms 42–72;
- Book 3: Psalms 73–89;
- Book 4: Psalms 90–106; and
- Book 5: Psalms 107–150.

There are some identifiable groupings of psalms around specific themes, and it is helpful to understand the overall context when we study one particular psalm within any one of these groupings. For example:

- the focus of Psalms 93–100 is on the Lord as the great King;
- Psalms 113–118 form the Hallel, traditionally sung on Passover night;
- Psalms 120–134 are the 'songs of ascents' for pilgrims; and
- Psalms 146–150 close out the book with songs of praise.

Recurring themes

Some powerful themes recur though the psalms: the sovereignty, justice and faithful love of God; why evil people seem to prosper; personal trust and commitment to the promises of God in the face of difficulty; and the greatness of the power of the Creator God – the rock, the refuge, the fortress and the one worthy of our trust, our praise and our worship.

There is also some repetition of words and phrases and even of some whole psalms. For example:

- Psalm 53 is the same as Psalm 14 apart from a few details and the greater part of verse 5 of Psalm 53;
- Psalm 70 is practically identical to Psalm 40:13–17; and
- Psalm 108 is made up of two psalm endings: 57:7–11 and 60:5–12.

Style

The psalms are poetry and songs. Many contain poetic imagery. They include praise, thanksgiving, questioning, requests and laments, but rarely instruction.

Some psalms are written in the form of acrostics. For example, in the very long Psalm 119 each section begins with a different letter of the Hebrew alphabet. In Psalm 34 each verse begins with a different letter.

Who wrote the psalms?

Many of the psalms tell us (in their header) who wrote them. 73 of the 150 psalms are attributed to David, the shepherd boy who became king. Several were written by Asaph, a temple musician, and some by the Sons of Korah, a guild of temple officials. Others are attributed to authors such as Solomon (Ps. 72) and Moses (Ps. 90), or are unattributed (for example, Ps. 1).

When were the psalms written?

The simple answer seems to be over a period between the time of David (1000 BC approximately) – though with the psalm attributed to Moses possibly earlier – and the years after the exile of the people of Judah into Babylon (300–500 BC). In some cases the headers tell us about the circumstances in which the psalms were written. For example, the note at the head of Psalm 51 tells us that David's famous prayer of repentance was a response to God after the prophet Nathan had confronted him with his sins of adultery and murder. Similarly, we are told that David wrote Psalm 3 while on the run from his own son Absalom who was trying to kill him.

The psalms in the New Testament

The psalms formed the 'hymnbook' of Israelite religion before the time of Christ. There are over 50 quotations from the psalms in the New Testament – more than any other Old Testament book. The frequent use of quotations from 'messianic psalms' in the book of Acts shows us how many of the psalms prophetically point to the coming Messiah and have a specific fulfilment in Jesus Christ. Jesus frequently quoted from the psalms as part of God's Word and as revealing truth about himself (see, for example, Luke 24:44).

The psalms in the Christian church

From the very beginning of the Christian church the psalms have been accepted as part of the divine revelation, and have been used widely in personal and corporate prayers and praise for the past two thousand years. As we read the psalms, therefore, with the New Testament in our hand, we can expect to learn more about Jesus.

The value and use of the psalms today

The psalms form part of our inspired Scripture. When we read them with an open, prayerful heart, we will find that the God who inspired them will continue to speak through them today. He speaks to us where we are at. He challenges us, encourage us, and stirs up our faith and commitment to him.

Like all good poetry, the psalms engage the heart and emotions as well as the mind. Their continuing widespread use in study, private prayer and communal worship is testament to their ongoing appeal to believers in every culture. Whatever our experience at any given time in the emotional spectrum, from elated joy to deep depression, we can find a psalm which echoes our experience. It's no wonder that at times when we find it hard to read or study other parts of the Bible – when we are tired, sick or depressed – it is to the psalms that we turn. They help us to pray, to worship and to reflect on God and our relationship with him.

As we read them, study them, pray them or sing them, our God delights to use them to reveal to us more about himself and to deepen our knowledge of him.

Studying the psalms with this guide

Read the psalm for the day and then the notes and questions contained in the study guide. Ask yourself some questions as you read:

- What do I learn about God in this verse and passage?
- What did this mean to the original hearers?
- What does it mean for me in the twenty-first century?
- How can I respond with practical action?

DAY 1

Repentance and renewal

When we do something wrong, we might regret what we have done, or at least regret being found out! If we have damaged another person, we might also express remorse at the hurt we have caused. According to the Bible, repentance goes much deeper than regret and remorse. This very moving psalm of David shows us what repentance means, and how it leads to restoration and renewal. The background is David's double sin of adultery and conspiracy to murder, told in 2 Samuel 11 and 12.

Repentance

David had been courageously confronted with his wrongdoing by the prophet Nathan and was deeply troubled. Loaded down with guilt, he struggles to come to terms with the fatal flaw in his make-up that had caused him to do such evil. He knew what he had done was wrong, but he did it anyway. He had flouted God's authority, broken God's law and rejected his love (v. 4). So he acknowledges and confesses that he is fundamentally sinful (v. 5).

Seeking and receiving forgiveness is the start of restoration in any relationship. So it is in our relationship with God. David seeks God's forgiveness. He asks God to 'blot out' (v. 1) his transgressions, to 'wash away' (v. 2) his iniquity, which was spoiling and defiling him, and to 'cleanse' (v. 2) him from sin. He acknowledges that something has to change radically in his life .

Renewal

David desperately wants a new start. He wants to be clean (v. 7), to be a new person, with even the memory of past failures forgotten and totally forgiven. He wants to experience the re-creative power of God in his life (v. 8) and the conscious, constant presence of God (v. 11), and for God to restore the joy which he had lost (v. 12). He also prays that God would again use him to help others find their way back to God (v. 13).

REFLECTION

David confessed his sin, faced up to the sinfulness of his nature, realised he had offended God, then sought God's forgiveness and God's grace and power to change his life. That's what repentence means (1 John 1:8–9).

DAY 2

READ Psalm 52

Two ways to live

This psalm presents two contrasting ways to live. Doeg's deceit, self-serving and violence is contrasted with David's trust in God. David was on the run from Saul, staying with Ahimelek, the priest (1 Sam. 22:6–22). Doeg, the Edomite, had told Saul where David was hiding (1 Sam. 22:9). When Ahimelek refused to betray David, Doeg killed Ahimelek and then slaughtered 85 innocent priests, along with their wives, children and animals (1 Sam. 22:18–19).

'The mighty man' (vv.1–4)

David addresses Doeg directly (vv. 1–4). Using irony and sarcasm, he calls him a 'mighty hero' (v. 1), just as we might sarcastically label someone who preys on the elderly and disabled with, 'What a 'hero!' or, 'What a bigshot!' In reality Doeg is 'a disgrace in the eyes of God' (v. 1). He is deceitful; he loves the whole business of lying and scheming to deceive and outwit the vulnerable (vv. 2–4).

No future (v. 5)

David sees clearly the future of Doeg and all those like him. Those who have no regard for God, and who grow strong by destroying others (v. 7), will themselves be destroyed. Those who boast of their power (v. 1) will themselves become an object of derision (v. 6). God will bring them down to 'everlasting ruin' (v. 5). They may plot, scheme and kill, but it is they who have no future.

The contrast

David affirms his continuing trust in 'God's unfailing love' (v. 8). Strong in this faith, David pictures two trees. One is cut down, like Doeg (v. 5). The other, like David, is 'an olive tree flourishing in the house of God' (v. 8), fruitful and durable.

REFLECTION

Doeg epitomises all those in every generation who use whatever trickery, deceit or violence is needed to further their own interests. When we are confronted with violence and deceit in the daily news bulletins or in our own experience, let's hold firmly to the truth of verse 5 and make our stand like David (vv. 8–9).

(Note: as Psalm 53 is almost identical to Psalm 14, no separate study is provided.)

DAY 3

READ Psalm 54

Dealing with betrayal

Being let down by anyone is a painful experience. Far worse is being 'stabbed in the back' by a friend or family member you thought you could trust. Such situations test our faith. In this psalm we are given an insight into David's experience of betrayal and how he was able to come through it with even stronger confidence in God's unfailing love.

In Psalm 52, David had been betrayed by Doeg, an Edomite and therefore a natural enemy. But here it was the Ziphites, people from David's own tribe, who told Saul where David was in hiding (1 Sam. 23:19–20; 26:1).

David prays ... (vv. 1–3)

David's life was in danger. Saul was after him because he was jealous of David's success and popularity. Later, when David confronted Saul, he asked him, 'Why is my lord pursuing his servant? What have I done, and what wrong am I guilty of?' (1 Sam 26:18). So, as David prays here to God for help, he also asks God to vindicate him (v. 1).

... And puts the situation in God's hands (vv. 4–5)

David had a small band of brave and loyal men (1 Sam. 23:13; 2 Sam. 23:8–39), but recognises that without the Lord's help he would not have survived (v. 3). He prays for God to deal with his enemies. Twice he had the opportunity to kill Saul (see 1 Sam. 24 and 26), but would not take it out of respect for Saul's office as 'the LORD's anointed' (2 Sam. 24:6). So he prays for God to take vengeance rather than David acting himself (see also Rom. 12:19).

David continues to trust in God as his mighty helper (v. 4). He commits to praising God (v. 6) and puts his hope in the name of God (v. 4). He also makes a point of intentionally thanking God for deliverance in answer to prayer (v. 7).

REFLECTION

The New Testament tells us how Jesus, like David, was pursued by enemies without cause, betrayed by a close friend, but did not take revenge: 'When they hurled their insults at him, he did not retaliate ... Instead, he entrusted himself to him who judges justly' (1 Pet. 2:23).

DAY 4

Praying and trusting

Learning how to pray is a lifelong experience. Learning to trust God in the face of worries, family crises, fear and uncertainty is another. This psalm shows us David being honest with God, 'telling it like it is'. But he is keeping his focus on God and on God's willingness to listen to David's prayers and to save him from his enemies (vv. 1, 16). The psalm begins with prayer (v. 1) and ends with trust (v. 23).

Trouble

David has had enough. He wants to escape: 'Oh, that I had the wings of a dove! I would fly away and be at rest' (v. 6). He is in danger and very much afraid of personal attack (vv. 2–5). As he looks at the city he lives in, he sees nothing but evil at work: violence, strife, malice, abuse, destructive forces, threats and lies (vv. 9–11). Turning back to his own problems, he remembers his deep disappointment and disillusionment with some of his closest friends who had let him down when he needed them most (vv. 12–14).

Prayer

How does David respond? He prays throughout the day: 'Evening, morning and noon' (v. 17). He shares with us his very personal prayers (vv. 16–18). He is confident that God will hear and will humble his enemies (v. 19), but then he remembers again the betrayal by his friends which had hurt him very badly (vv. 20–21). As he continues to pray, he rests in the confidence that God will sort out the situation with justice (v. 23). He takes his problems to the Lord in prayer and shares with us this wonderful encouragement: 'Cast your cares on the LORD and he will sustain you; he will never let the righteous be shaken' (v. 22).

REFLECTION

Whatever the state of the world, however much he is let down by others and however he is feeling, David keeps praying: 'As for me, I call to God' (v. 16), and he keeps trusting: 'as for me, I trust in you' (v. 23). Whatever our situation, experience or mood, this is surely a good position to take.

DAY 5

READ Psalm 56

'In God I trust'

'It was like stepping through a minefield.' That's how a friend described a bad experience at work, trying to sort out difficult problems and not seeing clearly the right way forward. Life can sometimes feel like that. David was experiencing the same in this psalm.

He was on the run from King Saul and fled for safety to Gath, the stronghold of the Philistines, Israel's arch-enemy. Remember that David became a national hero through killing Goliath, the champion Philistine warrior, against all the odds. He would not exactly have been popular in the Philistine stronghold, so he must have been in a desperate state to go there. Not surprisingly, the Philistines were suspicious. David therefore felt threatened and feigned madness to escape (1 Sam. 21:10–15). In this situation he faced two different enemies at the same time: the Philistines, and Saul's men who were trying to kill him. This attack was also relentless – the phrase 'all day long' is used in verses 1 and 2.

What is David's response? First, he cries out to God (v. 1). Then, he stands his ground and makes his statement of faith: 'When I am afraid, I put my trust in you. In God, whose word I praise – in God I trust and am not afraid' (vv. 3–4). This memorable phrase is repeated again in verses 10–11.

His rhetorical question 'What can mere mortals do to me' (v. 4; see also v. 11) could be answered very simply: they could torture and kill him. His enemies were certainly out to get him (vv. 5–6). David was under enormous stress and very fearful. He asks God, 'Record my misery; list my tears on your scroll' (v. 8). It's in this crisis situation that he affirms his trust in God and in his word (v. 10)

Finally, David records with thankfulness that God answers prayer. God had protected and delivered him, and had brought him through this particular 'minefield' unscathed (vv. 12–13).

REFLECTION

Trust in the unseen God will always be tested in real-life situations. Turn back to Psalm 34 to understand more of David's trust in God in this nightmare experience.

DAY 6

READ Psalm 57

In the shadow of his wings

Have you ever wondered why David, who was clearly a very courageous man (remember he had singlehandedly fought and defeated Goliath), writes in the psalms about taking refuge in God? In this psalm, he pictures himself like a small bird sheltering under the wings of its mother (v. 1). Was David admitting to cowardice and weakness, always wanting to run away, unable to cope anymore?

Actually there is nothing cowardly about running to a refuge. Ask any mountain climber caught in a storm or any soldier outnumbered and caught in crossfire! Once inside the refuge there is a great feeling of relief and security. But when David speaks of God being his refuge (v. 1), he means more than just an impersonal shelter. He means being welcomed by a loving God (v. 10). Think how you might feel, arriving home after a particularly stressful day, to be welcomed by someone you love very much. As you shut the door and start to relax and unwind, you are thankful beyond words to be safely home. It's in that sense that we take refuge in God. It's not cowardice; it's being human.

David may be hiding from Saul in a cave, but he knows it is the Lord who is his real refuge. It is the Lord who shelters him under his wings until danger is past (v. 1). His sudden burst of praise (v. 5) sounds quite strange at first, sandwiched between two brutal reminders of his dangerous situation (vv. 4, 6). But, as we read the whole psalm, we see that this longing that God 'be exalted', repeated like a chorus in verses 5 and 11, divides the psalm into two parts:

- prayer for God's mercy and grace in the face of the threat from David's enemies (vv. 1–4); and
- turning to praise God whose love holds David's heart 'steadfast' in such frightening and unsettling circumstances (vv. 6–10).

REFLECTION

Why, when he has so many personal issues to deal with, do you think David longs so much for God to be recognised and worshipped everywhere (vv. 5, 11)?

Evil tyrants

When life is comfortable, it's easy to think that human nature is basically good. If we are enjoying a reasonably peaceful life, then concentration camps, genocide and terrorism may seem a long way away. Such things may not touch us. But when war crimes are reported, when cruel, power-hungry leaders are exposed by the media or when evil invades our comfortable lives, we are jolted out of our complacency. We are surprised and appalled at the horror that one human being can inflict on another. It makes us revise our opinion of human nature and to ponder how low human beings can sink, particularly given different circumstances and without God's grace.

This psalm speaks about evil and justice in a way which some may find offensive or even 'unchristian' (see for example vv. 7–10). The psalms, like the whole Bible, make clear that for justice to triumph the innocent must be acquitted and freed, and the guilty must be punished. These are the two sides of justice. Thank God he has created a moral universe, where the crimes of those who have tortured, imprisoned or killed innocent people will not go unpunished.

Here David confronts the tyrants, the rulers who 'devise injustice' and 'mete out violence on the earth' (v. 2). Evil has taken a hold in their lives from birth (v. 3) and their poison, like that of a cobra, does its lethal damage (vv. 4–5). So David unashamedly prays to God, 'Break the teeth in their mouths' and 'tear out the fangs of those lions!' (v. 6), and asks that these evil rulers would 'vanish like water that flows away' (v. 7).

David longs that justice will be done, and be seen to be done, so that people are reassured that 'the righteous still are rewarded' (v. 11) and evil destroyed. Then everyone will see that 'there is a God who judges the earth' (v. 11).

REFLECTION

Let's thank God for his justice and his mercy. Let's pray and work for justice, tempered with mercy, in our society.

DAY 8

READ Psalm 59

'My God on whom I can rely'

Who can you really rely on? When the chips are down, when you need help, when you need someone to 'be there for you', who among your family and friends do you turn to?

In this psalm, David is again in danger. Saul had sent men round to his house to kill him and Michal, his wife, had helped him to escape through a window (1 Sam. 19:11–17). But David sees a bigger picture. It is God who watches over him and delivers him. David relied on Michal on this occasion, but he was to be betrayed and let down many times in his life. He knew that in the final analysis he could only rely fully on God.

As David prays for deliverance (vv. 1–2), he draws God's attention to the band of men who conspire against him (vv. 3, 14–15) and calls on God to intervene (vv. 4–7). Notice how David's thoughts move from himself – 'me' and 'I' (vv. 1, 2, 4) – to 'they', his enemies – described with increasing intensity (vv. 3, 6–7, 14–15) – to 'you ... LORD' (vv. 5, 8–10, 17).

David, the Lord's newly anointed king, was being threatened by King Saul, whose actions and behaviour had disqualified him from being fit for office. With the whole Bible in our hand, we can see a bigger picture here. We are reminded of how Herod, a later 'nominal' king of Judea and a man also unfit to hold the office, conspired with Pilate to get rid of Jesus, the true King of Israel. But they were only allowed to do what God had decided beforehand should happen (Acts 2:25–29). They could not defeat the plan and purpose of God (see Ps. 2:4 and 59:8).

REFLECTION

David was at home when Saul's men came to get him. Even his home was not a refuge, but a place of danger. God was his only refuge (a place of safety) and his fortress (a place secure against attack). For David, as for us, this loving God is also the source of his strength to keep going (vv. 16–17).

God's help in a crisis

King David was in trouble. He was having to fight battles on two fronts at the same time.

The story is told in 2 Samuel 8:1–14 and 1 Chronicles 18:1–13. It was while David was away fighting in the north of the country that Edom, his old enemy, had taken the opportunity to attack from the south.

David pleads with God to get the people out of their mess, which the Lord himself seems to have brought upon them: 'You have rejected us ... you have been angry ... You have shaken the land ... You have shown your people desperate times' (vv. 1–3). David cries out to God: 'now restore us!' (v. 1). The land has been invaded and 'torn ... open' (v. 2). David is faced not just with the attacks from his enemies but with the deeper worry that God had rejected his people and will 'no longer go out with our armies?' (v. 10).

So David appeals for God to help and save them (v. 5). His appeal is based on the unchanging love and strength of God (v. 5) and on God's sovereignty – the land belongs to God (vv. 6–9). David also confesses that they are not going to get out of this mess with their own strength and resources: 'human help is worthless' in this situation (v. 11). It is only 'With God we shall gain the victory' (v. 12).

David dispatched Joab, his army commander, to the south to defeat the Edomites and repel the invasion (see the header to this psalm), but Scripture gives the credit to David as the Lord's anointed king: 'The LORD gave David victory wherever he went' (2 Sam. 8: 6, 14).

REFLECTION

The header to this psalm tells us it is 'For teaching', that is, there are lessons to be learned here. First, when trouble surrounds us on all sides, let's remember that God is still in control. Second, we shouldn't forget that we can call on him for help; we can rely on his love and his strength. Third, we learn that it is when we are totally relying on God, seemingly at our weakest, that we are truly strong (2 Cor. 12:9).

Shelter, safety, and security

David is far from home, or at least he feels as though he is: 'O God ... From the ends of the earth I call to you' (vv. 1–2). He is also feeling 'faint' of heart (v. 2), overwhelmed by the challenges he faces and unable to cope. So he cries out to God.

Let's notice the progression of different word pictures that David uses in this prayer for the shelter and security he finds in God. First, there is the familiar picture of the rock (v. 2), high on the hill, a natural vantage point from which to see his enemies and a hard place for them to attack.

Second, there is the refuge tower (v. 3), a human-made place of safety. Recently I visited the Wicklow Mountains in Ireland where I saw a high stone tower built by monks in the tenth century as a place of safety when they were attacked. The entrance door was three metres above the ground. The monks, I was told, would climb into the tower using a ladder, pull up the ladder behind them, shut the door and were safe!

Third, there is the tent (v. 4), which may seem a far more vulnerable shelter until we remember that the tent (that is, the tabernacle) was the place where the people met with the Lord as they travelled across the wilderness (Ex. 40:34–38).

Fourth, there is safety 'in the shelter of your wings' (v. 4), a deeply relational image we have seen before (Ps. 57:1).

So we move from the high rocky outcrop to the tower, to the tent, to the shelter of the wings – a progression, it seems, of increasing vulnerability. But, in biblical terms, it is a progression of increasing safety and of an increasingly deep, personal relationship.

REFLECTION

This world is a very unsafe and uncertain place. Let's look to find our shelter in God, in a relationship with him through faith in Jesus Christ, the King who is prefigured here in David's prayer (vv. 6–7). Is there anywhere safer in this world than being 'in Christ' in the presence of this loving, faithful God (v. 7)?

Quiet trust in a crisis

Sometimes our troubles drive us away *from* God. This psalm of David encourages us to let them drive us *to* him.

The opening line, 'Truly my soul finds rest in God' (v. 1), has a strong sense of waiting in reverential silence before God. David can rest in faith: no words need be spoken. The phrase is repeated in verse 5, though this time with David speaking to himself, encouraging himself to keep resting and trusting in God.

David is under intense pressure from people trying to bring him down (vv. 3–4). He is feeling like a 'leaning wall' and 'a tottering fence', about to collapse completely. But, as he considers the pressure he is under and the opposition arrayed against him, he affrms strongly his trust in God who is his salvation (v. 7) and, as in Psalm 61, his rock, fortress and refuge (vv. 6–8).

Having encouraged himself, David then turns to encourage all of us who read this psalm to trust God for ourselves and to 'pour out' our hearts to him (v. 8). He reminds us that life is short (v. 9) and that acquiring wealth through dishonest means is a fool's game (v. 10), because at the end we all have to give account to God (v. 12). Valuing too highly our supposed position in society is also to live an illusion, because that also is as fleeting as a breath. It is God who is truly powerful (v. 11), and it is his love which lasts and does not fail.

When crises come for us, as they did for David, there is no lasting security without God. It is not that God is there for us only when we decide to turn to him. He is the *only* rock, and all other support systems we rely on will eventually prove to be inadequate.

REFLECTION

This psalm shows us that there is a time for silent waiting before God, a time to call on God, a time to pour out our hearts to him and a time to remind ourselves, and others, of all that he is for us.

Devotion to God

If you love someone, it's good to tell them so – to express in words how much you love them, respect them and appreciate their care for you. When you are apart, you tell them by whatever means you can how much you want to be back with them. How much more do we need to express our love and devotion to God like that!

This psalm is one of pure devotion. David longs with all his heart to be closer to God. His relationship with God is the most precious thing in his life: 'You, God, are my God ... I thirst for you, my whole being longs for you' (v. 1). This thirst to know God is a longing with great singleness of purpose. When we are *really* thirsty, only water will do – not coffee, spirits, wine or juice. When we long for God, only knowing his presence in our lives will satisfy us. No other substitutes will do.

Feeling spiritually 'dried out', David first *looks back* to experiences of God's presence and power, now gone but not forgotten: 'I have seen you in the sanctuary and beheld your power and your glory' (v. 2). Then, he reaffirms his belief in the unfailing and unchanging love of God as a *present reality*: 'your love is better than life' (v. 3). He meditates on God and worships God even in the waking moments of the night (vv. 6–7). He is confident that his enemies will be destroyed (vv. 9–10). Finally, because of God's love, David commits himself to continuing to praise and honour God *in the future*: 'my lips will glorify you. I will praise you as long as I live' (vv. 3–4).

REFLECTION

Looking back with thankfulness, looking forward with hope and living in the present sticking closely to God (v. 8) – what a great way to live!

DAY 13

READ Psalm 64

When the enemy looms large

When one of my daughters was little, she picked up a telescope the wrong way round and pointed it at me. 'Daddy, you look very small and far away,' she said.

Some days God may seem far away. Our problems loom large and we feel overwhelmed by the evil in the world. We need to get our telescope the right way round.

This psalm reminds us that whatever our moods or feelings, the unseen realities do not change. Almighty God is in charge, but we are to keep alert and watch out for the evil one who may attack us 'like a roaring lion' (1 Pet. 5:8–9), who speaks with a very persuasive voice (Matt. 4:1–11; 16:22–23) and who can even appear as 'an angel of light' (2 Cor. 11:14). We are called to resist him, firm in our faith

In Psalm 63, the focus was on God, with the enemy mentioned almost as an afterthought. Here, in Psalm 64, the king's enemies are front and centre (vv. 1–6). They scheme and plot against the king (v. 2). They use 'cruel words' as 'deadly' weapons (v. 3) and attack innocent people without fear or conscience (v. 4). They work together to cover up their plans (v. 5) and plot injustice against innocent people (v. 6).

If that is where the psalm stopped, if that is all there was to say, we would have no hope. But the hinge on which the psalm turns is in two short words: 'But God ... (v. 7).

When God opens our eyes to understand that he is far more powerful than all the evil in the world, and greater than the evil in our own heart (1 John 4:4), then this realisation will be the turning point in our experience also. Evil is all around, but Jesus won the crucial battle with the powers of darkness when he died for our sins (Col. 2:15). One day the war will be over (vv. 7–8). And the result? Others will see and proclaim the works of God, take refuge in him and glory in him (vv. 9–10).

REFLECTION

Though we have to fight spiritual battles every day, God's final, future victory is certain (vv. 9–10) and we, by God's grace, will share in it.

DAY 14

READ Psalm 65

Harvest time

At last! After so many laments reflecting David's very troubled life comes a song of praise to God, a song of thankfulness, most probably a special thanksgiving for a great harvest, which is the main theme of the last five verses.

The psalm opens with God in his temple and David renewing his vows of commitment (v. 1). He had come to God in repentance and found forgiveness for his sins (v. 3). Knowing that God had forgiven him, he is no longer overwhelmed by sin (v. 3), but amazed at the privilege of being invited to come to worship God and to know him (v. 4).

Then, his gaze expands beyond himself and the temple surroundings to worship the God who is the hope of all the earth (v. 5). God is greater than the mountains which appear so secure (v. 6), greater than the restless seas (v. 7) and greater than all the chaos and conflict between the peoples of the world (v. 7).

Finally, David turns to reflect on the goodness of God in his creation (vv. 9–13). God sends rain for the crops (v. 10), provides for the people (v. 9) and for the herd of cattle and flocks of sheep (vv. 12–13). David is very thankful for his daily bread. He is overwhelmed by God's generosity in providing for him and for his people. The land is enriched 'abundantly' and the streams are 'filled' (v. 9). The year is crowned with his 'bounty' and the grain carts 'overflow' (v. 11).

He is the gracious God who forgives us and calls us to come to him to know him. He is the awesome Creator God of all the earth who provides all we need. Isn't he worthy of our worship? Should we not thank him every day we live? For he is the giver of 'Every good and perfect gift' (Jas. 1:17).

REFLECTION

As we read this psalm, we find some similar themes to those in the Lord's Prayer which Jesus taught us: our need of forgiveness, our need of daily food and the reminder to lift our eyes to see that the kingdom, the power and the glory belong not to us, but to our Father in heaven.

DAY 15

READ Psalm 66

A testimony to 'what God has done'

What do you say when you have the opportunity to give an account of your faith in Christ, whether in conversation with a friend or speaking in public? Do you talk mostly about yourself and your personal experience and understanding of God, or about something more?

This psalm of thanksgiving is a beautifully balanced testimony to what God has done, in history and in the psalmist's own life. It reminds us that our testimony, that is our witness to others about the reality of God and the truth of his Word, will always have these two parts. First, what God has done in history, as recorded in the Bible, through the life, death and resurrection of our Lord Jesus Christ. Second, what God has done in our own lives.

If we only recount the Bible facts, then our words lack any grounding in personal experience. On the other hand, if we only talk about ourselves, we divert attention away from our Lord and Saviour and from the Word of God on which our faith is based.

This psalm invites us, 'Come and see ...' (v. 5) and, 'Come and hear ...' (v. 16). It begins with a call to 'all the earth' to praise God for his name (vv. 1, 4), signifying his covenant promises and holy character, and to praise God for his powerful deeds (vv. 3, 5). The psalmist exhorts us, 'Come and see what God has done ...' (v. 5). He looks back to the deliverance of God's people from Egypt (vv. 6–7) and testifies to the way God kept them, disciplined them and finally brought them to 'a place of abundance' (v. 12).

But he does much more than just recount past stories and state the Israelites' accepted beliefs about God. He makes his personal commitment of faith (vv. 13–15). He also shares what God has done in his own life (v. 16). Top of the list are that when he repented of his sin, God forgave him (v. 18), answered his prayers (v. 19) and continued to love him (v. 20).

REFLECTION

What is your testimony to what God, in Christ, has done for you? (1 Pet. 3:15).

DAY 16

READ Psalm 67

A blessing to others

Think of those people who have been a blessing to you: those who shared the gospel with you and taught you about Jesus; those who prayed for you, gave you a Bible or helped you when you needed it most. Just thinking about them may bring a smile to your face. In the words of Proverbs, 'The memory of the righteous is a blessing' (Prov. 10:7, ESV). God blessed them, and you in turn were blessed through their life and witness. It is God's way. It goes right back to the time of Abraham: 'I will bless you ... and you will be a blessing ... all peoples on earth will be blessed through you' (Gen. 12: 2–3).

This psalm is a prayer that God's people will be a blessing to the nations (vv. 1–2). This was, and still remains, God's purpose for his people in every age: to pass on what we have received (Matt. 28:18–20; Rom, 10:9–15), and to live so that other people are blessed and God is honoured and glorified (Matt. 5:16). God uses people who have come to know him through faith in Jesus Christ to spread the knowledge of him around the world.

So we can join the psalmist in praying: 'may all the peoples praise you. May the nations be glad and sing for joy' (vv. 3–4). He understands that God's blessing of the nations will include both salvation (v. 2) and justice (v. 4), a setting to rights of all wrongs.

The psalm ends with a reference to the harvest as a sign of God's tangible blessing (see also Ps. 65), but it comes with a prayer that goes way beyond thanksgiving for local prosperity. It has a much wider vision. It's another 'so that' prayer (like v. 2): 'May God bless us still, *so that* all the end of the earth will fear him' (v. 7, my italics).

REFLECTION

Jesus calls us to come to him and find forgiveness and new life. He also calls us to bear fruit – fruit that will last and fruit that blesses others (John 15:5, 8, 16).

DAY 17

READ Psalm 68

Do it again, Lord

What are we to make of this psalm? It's different to many of the prayers and laments we have seen so far. It pictures God on the march (v. 7), leading his people from Mount Sinai through the wilderness, into the Promised Land, and on into the sanctuary in Jerusalem (see 2 Sam. 6:12).

Like Psalm 44, it *looks back* to God's work in the past. It *looks around* to a rather less glorious present, but also looks to God Almighty, *El Shaddai* (v. 14), the covenant-keeping 'LORD' (v. 4) who has not changed. Then, *looking to the future*, the psalmist effectively prays, 'Lord, please do it again' (v. 28).

The psalm begins with prayer for God to arise and 'blow ... away' his enemies (vv. 1–2). It celebrates God's victorious march from Egypt to Jerusalem (vv. 7–18). It was God who led them. He was present with his people all the way: 'the LORD has come from Sinai into his sanctuary' (v. 17). Then, in verses 25–31, we join the singers and musicians in a great procession to celebrate God's victory.

In between, we are given some beautiful cameos of the character of God, who:

- cares for the orphans, the widows and the lonely (vv. 5–6);
- saves his people and 'daily bears our burdens' (vv. 19–20);
- is awesome in his power (vv. 32–35);
- will destroy his enemies (vv. 14, 21); and
- 'gives power and strength to his people' (v. 35).

But it is verse 28 and the verses following which express the deep longing of the psalmist: 'Summon your power, God; show us your strength, our God, as you have done before' (v. 28). We too might pray today, 'Lord, as you worked in the past in your church and in our lives, please do it again!'

REFLECTION

This is a psalm for days when evil seems to be on the march and winning on all fronts. The Bible reminds us that God's final victory is certain, so we can celebrate that – and enjoy a foretaste of it now. God's greatest work was in the cross of Christ, where we see God's power and God's wisdom (1 Cor. 1:23–24).

DAY 18

READ Psalm 69

Crying out for help

Why are so many of David's psalms desperate prayers for God's help? Is it common human experience to have more bad days than good? Was that David's experience? Is it (more profoundly) a prophetic insight into the truth that God's anointed king would suffer? As Jesus himself explained, 'Did not the Messiah have to suffer these things and then enter his glory?' (Luke 24:26).

As we read the psalms, God surely means us to see David (the anointed king) prefiguring the coming Messiah (Jesus, God's Son) in his royal calling and in his suffering (see for example Ps. 2, 16, 22 and 110). The New Testament applies this psalm to Jesus in quoting verse 9 (John 2:17 and Rom. 15:3) and verse 21 (Matt. 27:34, 48).

But Paul also applies this psalm to us through Christ (Rom. 15:1–3). So we can read this too as the experience of the suffering of God's people in every generation (Phil. 3:10). Many of us have prayed prayers like Psalm 69 at one time or another: 'Save me, O God, for the waters have come up to my neck. I sink in the miry depths, where there is no foothold' (vv. 1–2).

David was at the end of his tether and in fear for his life. He prayed, but it looked like God was no longer listening (v. 3). He was surrounded by enemies (v. 4). Inside, he was a mass of guilt and shame (v. 5). His family had rejected him (v. 8). He was also an object of abuse and bad jokes for the local drunks (v. 12). But David had not given up praying. Neither had he given up trusting in the goodness and faithfulness of God. There is a turning point in this psalm when he prays and appeals to the Lord, in his great, unchanging, steadfast love (vv. 13, 16), to rescue him 'from the mire' (v. 14).

REFLECTION

David's focus on God in prayer moves on to praise and confidence that God will keep his promises and not leave David when he needs God most (vv 30–36).

(Note: as Psalm 70 is almost identical to Psalm 40:13–17, no separate study is provided.)

DAY 19

READ Psalm 71

God's lifelong care

'Old age is not for cissies.' Those words, widely attributed to the Hollywood actor Bette Davis, have been echoed by many. The writer of this psalm was approaching old age, but found that life wasn't getting easier. Instead of enjoying comfortable retirement, he was still fighting off his enemies. Sensing the weakness of one who looked past his use-by-date, those enemies were now closing in for the kill (vv. 10–11). How does the psalmist deal with this double problem of ageing and increased pressure?

First, he affirms strongly, in words very like Psalm 31, his faith in God as his refuge, his rock, his fortress, his protector and his place of security (vv. 1–3). He asks God to deliver him from 'the grasp of those who are evil and cruel' (v. 4).

Then, looking back over his life, he recalls that the Sovereign Lord has been his hope and confidence since his youth (v. 5). Indeed, he can't remember a time when he has not relied on God (v. 6). But now he is fearful of what old age will bring. In particular he is afraid that God might leave him and disown him. Twice he expresses this fear (vv. 9, 18).

As so often in the psalms, the turning point comes about halfway through when the psalmist takes his stand: 'As for me, I shall always have hope; I will praise you more and more' (v. 14). He now focuses on things he yet wants to accomplish, namely to testify to the next generation about God (v. 18). He wants to speak to all who will listen about God's righteousness, his salvation and his mighty acts (vv. 15–18, 24).

Finally, he turns to the God who has cared for him throughout his life and reflects that God is good: 'Though you have made me see many troubles … you will restore my life again … You will increase my honour and comfort me once more' (vv. 20–21).

REFLECTION

The psalmist relied totally on the faithful God and was committed to praising him (vv. 6, 14, 22–23) and to telling others of his might acts – what a great way to live purposefully in old age!

DAY 20

A king greater than Solomon

This psalm is a magnificent prayer for the king. The psalm is headed 'Of Solomon', so it could be a prayer by Solomon (David's son) for himself or for a later king who was to follow him, or possibly it is a prayer by David. Whichever it is, the focus is on the qualities that the Lord's anointed king should display, in his character and his actions, as the one entrusted by God with leadership of God's people. A quick reading of the Old Testament book of Kings tells us that, with a couple of notable exceptions (for example, Hezekiah and Josiah), the kings that followed spectacularly failed to live up to this ideal.

This psalm paints a picture of the qualities of the ideal king:

- he will judge with justice (v. 2) so that the righteous will flourish – always a sign of a just society;
- he will bring prosperity and will bless the people, as showers of rain refresh a newly mown field (v. 6; in contrast King Solomon himself failed to do this, 1 Kgs. 12:4);
- he will 'defend the afflicted' and 'save the children of the needy' (v. 4), crushing those who oppress them; he will deliver the most vulnerable and 'rescue them from oppression and violence' (vv. 12–14);
- his reign will last as long as the sun and moon (v. 5), just as Isaiah prophesied the coming Messiah's reign would have no end (Is. 9:7); and
- he will rule over the whole earth (vv. 8–11); all the kings will bow to him (v. 11) and all nations will be blessed through him (v. 17; see Phil. 2:11).

This portrait of the ideal king foreshadows King Jesus, who was greater than Solomon (Luke 11:31) and greater than David. King Jesus is the one who uniquely, fully, revealed God's character to us in his life, death and resurrection.

REFLECTION

Verse 20 tells us, 'This concludes the prayers of David son of Jesse.' This is the last of the psalms in Book 2, which ends appropriately with praise (vv. 18–19). We might join the psalmist in praising God for his justice, his love and his tender care of the needy, and ask God that our lives will display the same qualities.

DAY 21

READ Psalm 73

Tested faith[1]

The writer of this psalm was on a slippery slope. He was comparing himself to others – to those who seemed to defy God and yet still do very well in life – and concluding that he was getting a raw deal.

The psalmist begins, 'Surely God is good to Israel, to those who are pure in heart.' Then he shares his very personal experience of having this conviction tested. He looks in three directions.

First, as he *looks around*, he sees people who appear to be successful and free from care. They seem to have dispensed with religion and they mock the existence of God, yet they experience no ill effect (vv. 4–11). Indeed, they appear to be 'always free of care, they go on amassing wealth' (v. 12). As the psalmist struggles with the implications of this observation, he feels that his faith is failing as he has begun to envy 'the prosperity of the wicked' (vv. 2–3).

Then, he *looks inwards* at his own life (vv. 13–16). His faith and self-discipline seem to have brought no rewards, but rather the opposite (v. 14) . He wonders if his faith and religious practice have all been a waste of time. But he is reluctant to express these doubts aloud because he doesn't want to drag others down with him (v. 15).

Finally, he *looks to God* (vv. 17–27). Verse 17 is a turning point. His downwards slide is stopped when he starts to worship God. In that experience God reminds him of eternity and of the future destruction of all these seemingly successful people (v. 19). He remembers the presence of God and the promises of God to be always with him (vv. 24–25).

His mind is cleared and he gets things back in proportion. He realises that though his faith may waver, and his moods and emotions may go up and down, God remains the stronghold of his life (v. 26).

REFLECTION

'But as for me, it is good to be near God. I have made the Sovereign LORD my refuge; I will tell of all your deeds' (v. 28).

DAY 22

READ Psalm 74

Devastating defeat

When we suffer a major setback, when our hopes are dashed and our worst fears realised, we naturally ask, 'Why?' If there is a loving God, why has he allowed this to happen?

As we have seen, many of the psalms grapple with this question. In Psalm 13 it was an individual asking, 'Why?' Here it is the whole community. The Babylonian army had completely destroyed Jerusalem in 587 BC and left the nation devastated. God's people are asking why God has rejected them and allowed their enemies to humiliate them (vv. 1–8). They complain, 'We are given no signs from God; no prophets are left, and none of us knows how long this will be' (v. 9). God's people had been defeated, their holy place had been destroyed and their God was being laughed at (v. 10). Why had God seemingly abandoned his own people to their enemies (v. 11)?

Remember that these were the covenant people of God. He had made promises to them which he vowed never to break, but it looked like God had done exactly that. So they ask, 'O God, why have you rejected us forever? Why does your anger smoulder against the sheep of your pasture?' (v. 1).

But then the psalmist looks back to better times, when God *had* delivered his people, redeemed them and made them his own. He remembers that God is still in charge of his world (vv. 12–17). He realises that if God's people are being ridiculed, then so is God himself (vv. 18, 22). So he prays for the Lord to remember his covenant and to rise up in power against those who have inflicted such devastating misery on his own people (vv. 20–22).

As in Psalm 13, there is no direct answer to the question 'Why?' But in both prayers we find the writers finding some peace in remembering God (v. 1), together with his promises and how good he has been to them in the past (v. 2). They had forsaken him. But he had not rejected them 'for ever'.

REFLECTION

Even when we experience a seemingly devastating defeat, God's promises still provide solid ground on which to stand (2 Cor. 1:20).

DAY 23

READ Psalm 75

Who calls the shots?

We human beings have a great capacity for self-delusion. We can start to think we really run the show on this earth. We see our political leaders, the heads of big businesses and our best thinkers trying to convey an image of having the answers to the world's problem. We put celebrities and sporting heroes on a higher pedestal than most can bear. But then, thirty years later, most of them have faded from the spotlight. Another thirty years pass and all that remains is their ashes scattered to the wind.

We often hear 'experts', who like us have a short life span, speaking authoritatively about the origins of the universe without any reference to God the Creator. They assure us that all human problems can be solved without any need for God. This is self-aggrandisement and self-deception on a massive scale. It demonstrates an unrealistically high opinion of the powers of the human race. This psalm reminds us that there is a God who made the whole world and that it is he, not us, who calls the shots.

It is God who chooses the times (v. 2), who judges all and who holds the universe together (v. 3). So he rebukes those who speak defiantly against him. He warns them to stop boasting and to stop making a power play against the Almighty (vv. 4–5). We saw the same theme in Psalm 2. Then comes the reminder: 'It is God who judges: he brings one down, he exalts another' (v. 7). This is the key message of this psalm. It's one that Mary understood in her famous song (Luke 1:52). So did Hannah before her (1 Sam. 2:6–7).

The psalmist ends with a statement of personal commitment: 'As for me, I will declare this for ever, I will sing praise to the God of Jacob' (v. 9), who will put all things right in the end (v. 10).

REFLECTION

Here is another reminder that Almighty God is the one in charge of everything and we owe him our worship. See also Revelation 4:11.

DAY 24

Fear God

Near the summit of the Schilthorn, in the Swiss Alps, there is a small plaque engraved with these words, 'Fear God and give him glory, because the hour of his judgment has come ...' As visitors leave the cable car to be greeted by the awesome view of the surrounding mountain peaks, this text from Revelation 14:7 provides a very apt reminder of the awesome power of our Creator and of his coming judgement.

This psalm reminds us that God is to be feared. If we stand in awe of the powers in creation – in the ocean, wind, earthquakes and volcanic eruptions – how much more should we stand in awe of the Creator? Should we not also stand in awe and holy fear that this God has reached out in love to us? As Proverbs wisely says, 'The fear of the LORD is the beginning of wisdom' (Prov. 9:10).

Some psalms celebrate the worldwide sovereignty of God (see for example Ps. 8). This one begins by celebrating that God lives among his people. The psalm divides up like this:

- God is present among his people and honoured by them (vv. 1–2);
- God is victorious over his enemies (vv. 3–6) – perhaps a reference to God's miraculous rescue of Jerusalem from the attack of Sennacherib (Is. 47:36–37);
- God strikes the final blow against evil everywhere (vv. 7–9). The Judge of all the earth is also acknowledged as the King of all the earth, and at the end time those who commit themselves to God's keeping are saved (v. 9); and
- those rebelling against God finally submit to him (vv. 10–12).

All reading this psalm are therefore encouraged to make their own commitment to God, 'the One to be feared' (v. 11).

REFLECTION

Fear of God and loving God go together. Both are part of our faith relationship with him. See for example this beautiful balance in the New Testament: 'Then the church ... enjoyed a time of peace and was strengthened. Living* in the fear of the Lord *and encouraged by the Holy Spirit, it increased in numbers' (Acts 9:31,* my emphasis*).

DAY 25

READ Psalm 77

Look back and be encouraged

Sharing your deepest worries with a friend can be difficult, especially if they seem disinterested in what you have to say. You can tell by their body language that they aren't really listening. That's how the psalmist feels here. He is still believing and praying, but findng no comfort from God at all. It doesn't feel like God is even listening (vv. 1–4).

The psalmist is depressed, emotionally exhausted and unable to sleep (v. 2). He looks back to better times when God had worked in his life, when his nights were filled with song instead of fear and worry (vv. 5–6). But those days seem long past. As he ponders his situation, the psalmist asks himself six questions (vv. 7–9):

1. 'Will the Lord reject for ever?'
2. 'Will he never show his favour again?'
3. 'Has his unfailing love vanished for ever?'
4. 'Has his promise failed for all time?'
5. 'Has God forgotten to be merciful?'
6. 'Has he in anger withheld his compassion?'

He doesn't seem to get any answers, but the turning point in his experience comes in verse 10, where he appeals to the power of God. He then resolves to 'remember', 'consider' and 'meditate on' the ways that God worked in much darker times in the past (vv. 11–15).

In particular, he remembers how God led his people through the Red Sea. He describes this mighty act of God in striking poetic language (vv. 16–19). He remembers that God had led them *through*, not *around*, a seemingly impossible obstacle.

Finally, the psalmist remembers that in this great deliverance God's 'footprints were not seen' (v. 19). He was there, leading his people, by the hand of their human leaders, Moses and Aaron, but God himself remained unseen.

REFLECTION

When we are struggling to see why God has brought dark times to our life, when his presence seems far away and when we don't see his 'footprints', let's learn from this psalm. As we look back to God's work in the past in Jesus Christ – his death and resurrection – look up to God himself and look forward to the return of Christ, so we will be encouraged to trust God and press on.

DAY 26

Recovering from failure

Our failures don't take God by surprise. We may fail to achieve what we want to achieve or to be the people we want to be. We certainly all fail to be the people God wants us to be.

The Bible is full of examples of human failure. It doesn't airbrush its portraits of men and women of faith. They are shown as fallible people, but are still loved by God.

The failure of God's people

As the psalmist looks back over the history of God's people, he sees a recurring, threefold pattern of failure. They 'did not keep God's covenant and refused to live by his law'; they 'forgot' the wonderful things he had done for them (vv. 9–10). The people of Israel, who had been rescued by God from slavery in Egypt, then led through the Red Sea and across the desert, continued to sin against him. Indeed, 'They wilfully put God to the test' (v. 18). In spite of all God's goodness, 'they kept on sinning; in spite of his wonders, they did not believe' (v. 32). The result? 'So [God] ended their days in futility' (v. 33) – one of the saddest comments in all Scripture.

Learning from their failure

Why does the writer want to focus on this sad picture of failure? It isn't so that we would wallow in a pit of negativity. It is so that we would *learn* from their mistakes and not be like them (v. 8; see also 1 Cor. 10:1–13).

God's patience

Read this psalm again, but this time look at the patience of God rather than the failure of the people. Despite their failure and rebellion, God delivered them from their enemies, showed them his great power and provided for them when they were hungry. Best of all, he was merciful and forgiving (vv. 38–39).

REFLECTION

God knows we are likely to fail, and our churches are likely to fail. But whatever our failures – whatever we have done and however long we have neglected him – as we turn to him, he will again 'shine his face' upon us, forgive us and enable us to go forward with him. God faithfully keeps his promises even when we, his people, fail to keep ours (vv. 65–72).

DAY 27

READ Psalm 79

'For your name's sake ...'

Many Christian prayers end, '... for your name's sake.' They are familiar words, but what do they really mean? In the Bible, God's name is the revelation of his character. So when we ask God to answer and act 'for his name's sake', we are making a call on his love, mercy and faithfulness.

This psalm is an urgent plea to God for help in the face of a disaster, but underlying the prayer is a concern for God's name and reputation. After all, what sort of God would not protect his own people? Yet it appeared that God had failed to safeguard Israel.

The city of Jerusalem had been destroyed by the invading Babylonians. Their buildings had been ruined (v. 1), dead bodies were left lying in the streets (v. 2) and their blood had been 'poured out ... like water' (v. 3). It's a picture of the devastating effects of urban warfare, still familiar to us today.

For the people of Judah this situation felt far worse because they had claimed to be loved by God and protected by God. Yet the destruction of Jerusalem had been a long time coming. God had sent prophets like Jeremiah to warn his people of what would happen if they continued to ignore him and generally live as they pleased. But they hadn't listened.

As the psalmist prays for God's forgiveness (v. 9) and for God to rescue them from their desperate situation (v. 8), notice how he appeals to God's name and reputation. The nations have invaded '*your* inheritance' and defiled '*your* holy temple' (v. 1, my italics). Likewise, it is 'your servants' who have been killed (v. 2). He asks God to take vengeance on those who 'do not acknowledge you ... that do not call on your name' (v. 6). He asks God's help 'for the glory of your name' and for deliverance and forgiveness 'for your name's sake' (v. 9).

REFLECTION

When we pray for the Christian church and for the spread of the gospel, let's remember that it is Christ's church and Christ's gospel, and that it is his name that we carry.

DAY 28

READ Psalm 80

Hope of restoration

'Restore us, O God; make your face shine upon us, that we may be saved' (v. 3). This prayer is repeated twice, like a chorus of a song (vv. 7, 19).

This psalm begins with a prayer for the Lord, the 'Shepherd of Israel', to come to the rescue because the Shepherd's flock, the people of Israel, are in great danger (vv. 1–2).

The second stanza (vv. 4–6) begins by asking, 'How long, LORD God Almighty, will your anger smoulder against the prayers of your people?' (v. 4). God's people had endured the misery of defeat by their enemies, who were now laughing at them, but notice that the psalmist realises that this is the result of God's action in response to their rejection of him: 'You ... have made us an object of derision' (v. 6).

In the third stanza (vv. 8–18), the psalmist recalls that God had 'transplanted a vine from Egypt' (v. 8). He had redeemed an enslaved people and brought them into a land of their own. But now the nation of Israel had been destroyed. The vine had been 'cut down'.[2]

So the psalmist prays to God, 'Restore us' (v. 18; literally, 'return to us'), because it looked like he had left them. He pleads, 'revive us' (v. 18), because they were bereft of spiritual life. Finally, he asks, 'make your face shine on us' (v. 19), because they thought God had turned away.

The references to 'the man at your right hand, the son of man' (v. 17) seem to refer to the nation of Israel itself (see Hos. 11:1), but they also point forward to Jesus, the unique Son at God's right hand (Heb. 1:1–3) and the focus of our hope for revival and restoration.

REFLECTION

This psalm uses two pictures which recur throughout the Old Testament: the shepherd (vv. 1–7) and the vine (vv. 8–19). Not surprisingly we see the same themes in the New Testament where Jesus, the Son of God, is revealed as 'the good shepherd' (John 10:11) and 'the true vine' (John 15:1).

DAY 29

READ Psalm 81

'If only you would listen'

We may have heard our teachers or parents say this to us as children or adolescents. They told us what to do, but we thought we knew better. We did it 'our way' and got into trouble. Perhaps in exasperation they said to us, 'If only you would listen, this would not have happened!' God's call to his people to listen is the central message of this psalm (see vv. 8, 11, 13).

It begins with a song of praise, accompanied by musical instruments (vv. 1–4). Then, after *rejoicing*, it calls the people to look back and *remember* how the Lord delivered them from slavery in Egypt and 'removed the burden from their shoulders' (v. 6). He rescued them, spoke to them at Mt Sinai and tested them at Meribah (Ex.17:7; Num. 20:13). He told them plainly that they were to have no other gods (v. 9), a reminder of the first commandment, and called them to listen to and obey that instruction (v. 8). He promised to provide for them all they needed to eat and live (v. 10) ... *but* then comes the problem: 'But my people would not listen to me' (v. 11).

So God 'gave them over to their stubborn hearts to follow their own devices' (v. 12; see also Rom. 1:24, 26, 28). When the inevitable trouble followed, in the form of defeat by their enemies and lack of food, God appeals to them, 'If my people would only listen to me' (v. 13). If they would only listen, he would quickly subdue their enemies and provide them with all they need to live (vv. 14–16).

REFLECTION

This seems to be a lesson that we humans have great trouble in learning. We want God to listen to us when we pray, but we don't always want to listen to him. We want things our way and we suspect God is out to deny us enjoyment in life. The opposite is true. God wants to bless us with life in all its fullness (v. 16), if only we would listen to him. See also Matthew 13:9; Hebrews 3:7, 15; 4:7; Revelation 2:7.

DAY 30

READ Psalm 82

The one true God

Many of us live in pluralistic societies, where truth is relative and where all religions are considered to be of equal value. The Bible paints a very different picture. There is one true God who has revealed himself to us and who will hold the whole world to account.

This psalm portrays a picture of Almighty God presiding in the heavens over a courtroom in which other 'gods' are called to account (v. 1). 'Who are these other "gods?"' we might ask. The Bible has no place for polytheism. It seems to refer to the fallible human judges of Israel (see John 10:34–35) and 'the powers of this dark world ... the spiritual forces of evil in the heavenly realms' (Eph. 6:12.). These 'wannabee gods' spread evil, war and chaos in the world.

All these so-called 'gods' are called to account in God's courtroom. They promote injustice and favour corruption (v. 2). They have no regard for the weak, the poor, the oppressed or the needy (vv. 3–4). They actually 'know nothing, they understand nothing' (v. 5). They have an inflated sense of their own importance and a limited life (vv. 5–7). By contrast, the one true God is the judge of all (v. 8).

Jesus said of false prophets, 'By their fruit you will recognise them' (Matt. 7:16). In other words, their values and actions will eventually reveal what they are really like. We might say something similar about the false 'gods' worshipped in our world today. Do they produce cruelty and injustice, or exalt themselves? Then they are not of God, because he cares for justice, for the weak and defenceless, for the poor and the oppressed (vv. 3–4).

We cannot claim to know God and serve him if we don't value what he values. Eventually we become like the 'gods' we worship and our society becomes like the 'gods' it worships. But there is only one God.

REFLECTION

Think about the character of God revealed here (vv. 3–4). God's purpose is to change us into his likeness through the work of his Holy Spirit in our life (2 Cor. 3:18; Gal. 5:22–23).

DAY 31

READ Psalm 83

The Lord's enemies and the Lord's people

Many of the psalms describe the experience of being attacked by enemies. Is it that Israel's enemies are automatically God's enemies? Or that God's enemies are Israel's enemies? The two are not quite the same. The former smacks of all those who have gone to war convinced that they had God on their side. The latter speaks of the unchanging reality that God's enemies will oppose those who put their trust in him.

In the early days after Jesus' death and resurrection, Saul of Tarsus was leading the attacks on Christians. Then he was confronted by the risen Christ while travelling to Damascus (Acts 9). His life was changed. Saul thought he had God on his side when he was persecuting those claiming that Jesus was the Messiah. In reality, unknowingly, he was fighting against Christ himself, and therefore fighting against God. So Jesus challenged him: 'Saul, Saul, why do you persecute *me?*' (Acts 9:4, my italics). The Lord Jesus Christ was identifying totally with his people.

This psalm makes the close association between God and his people very clear. It's a prayer to God to see 'how *your* enemies growl, how *your* foes rear their heads' (v. 2). They 'conspire against *your* people' (v. 3). They want to wipe out the nation of Israel forever (v. 4). But their hatred of God's people is simply a manifestation of their enmity against God himself (see Ps. 2:1–3). Thus, 'they form an alliance against *you*' (v. 5).

Then the psalmist asks God to defeat them and destroy them as 'fire consumes the forest' (v. 14). But the psalmist has more in mind than victory and vengeance (vv. 9–15). He prays that God will open the eyes of his enemies in their shame of defeat 'so that they will seek your name' (v. 16). The psalmist ends by praying, 'Let them know that you ... alone are the Most High over all the earth' (v. 18).

REFLECTION

Jesus warns us to expect opposition simply because of our faith in him (John 15:18). He also promised that we will share in his victory (John 16:33).

DAY 32

READ Psalm 84

Settling priorities

Establishing priorities is good. Working out what we really value when 'the chips are down' is important. Our priorities are revealed in our character. What is truly important to us is shown in the way we spend our time and money; in our attitudes to our work and how we treat other people. Our priorities also shape who we are.

The writer of Psalm 84 tells us about his priorities. He longs above all else to be in the presence of God, with the people of God (vv. 1–2). He sees great blessing for those who live in God's presence and who find their strength in God (vv. 4–5). They make a difference for good to those around them and 'go from strength to strength' (vv. 6–7).

He shares his conviction about priorities in the way he spends his precious, God-given time: 'Better is one day in your courts than a thousand elsewhere' (v. 10). With all the different demands on his time, he concludes that one day in the presence of God is better than a thousand working, playing and relaxing without giving God a thought.

The psalmist also shares his conviction about the true value of the so-called important positions we often strive for: 'I would rather be a doorkeeper in the house of my God than dwell in the tents of the wicked' (v. 10). He would rather have a low position and be in right relationship with God, and enjoy fellowship with God's people, than take a top job if that would compromise his values. He expresses his conviction that he won't in some way miss out by putting God first because God is no one's debtor: 'The LORD bestows favour and honour' (v. 11).

REFLECTION

It's good to set priorities to help us manage our time, but best of all is settling once and for all that knowing God and serving him is our first priority: the one thing above all else that we value. Jesus said, 'seek first his [God's] kingdom and his righteousness, and all these things [our daily needs] will be given to you as well' (Matt. 6:33).

Revival

When our church is distracted with worries about buildings rather than people, more focused on organisational problems than growing in knowledge of God, and having very little impact on society, then we might long for God to revive us. When our lives get 'bogged down' in routine 'hassles' and worry, we might pray for God to renew our lives by his Spirit.

Like Psalm 80, this is a prayer for revival, but – as we shall see – the basis of the hope seems to go much deeper; the vision is wider. It begins, like many of the psalms, looking back to better times, when the Lord had restored them, forgiven them and 'covered' their sins (vv. 1–3). The psalmist prays to the Lord for restoration: 'Will you be angry with us for ever? (v. 5); 'Will you not revive us again?' (v. 6); 'Show us your unfailing love' (v. 7).

As he prays, the psalmist also commits himself to do what God's people had so often failed to do, namely to listen to God's Word and obey him (see Ps. 81). So he promises, 'I will listen to what God the LORD says ...' (v. 8).

Verses 9–13 give us one of the most beautiful summaries in all Scripture of the restoration of God's people to a right relationship with God and with the world. The picture is of harmony, or *shalom*: 'Love and faithfulness meet together; righteousness and peace kiss each other' (v. 10). These characteristics of God are the foundation of our relationship with him and at the core of all strong human relationships and societies. They remind us that God reaches out in love to make peace with lost sinners through the death of his Son: 'we have peace with God through our Lord Jesus Christ' (Rom. 5:1–2). Christ, the Righteous One, died for us and gives us peace.

In the poetry of this psalm, we see the earth and the heavens reaching towards each other in faithfulness and righteousness (v. 11). The tangible result is that the land yields a great harvest (v. 12) and God, graciously and victoriously, is on the move (v. 13) and calling us to follow.

REFLECTION

As we pray for God to revive and restore his church in the world, let's commit ourselves like the psalmist to listen to his voice and to centre our lives on his love and faithfulness (Prov. 3:3).

DAY 34

READ Psalm 86

An undivided heart

The heart of the problem

Little children have a very direct way of telling their parents what they want: 'I'm hungry!'; 'I'm tired!'; 'Can you carry me?' Sometimes our prayers to God have a similar directness and urgency. So it is with Psalm 86. In the first four verses there are five specific requests: 'Hear me'; 'Guard my life'; 'save your servant'; 'have mercy on me'; 'Bring joy'. More focused requests come later: 'Teach me your way'; 'Turn to me'; 'show your strength'; 'Give me a sign of your goodness' (vv. 11–17). David prays for a tangible sign that God is with him. But one specific request gets to the heart of the problem: he longs for 'an undivided heart' (v. 11).

Divided

David has come to God with a list of personal needs. But while praying he realises that he has one big problem, one that lies deep within himself. His heart is 'divided'; it's pulled in different directions. He wants to do the will of God, but he also wants to please himself. He feels this tension in his thinking, his decision-making and his actions. He longs to be whole (see also Jas. 1:6–7).

Wholeness

David begins this psalm down in the depths, but he ends on a very positive note. What causes the change? He ends his prayer, as we often do, with no definite answer, but he has consciously brought his *whole* life under the control of God. He prayed 'for an undivided heart' and he now moves forward confident that he will experience God's love and strength in his life (vv. 12–17).

REFLECTION

Notice all the reminders about the goodness of God in this psalm. God's solution to a divided heart is that he teaches us his way so that we walk in his truth, and that he unites our heart so that we might fear his name (v. 11). Let's ask him to do that!

DAY 35

READ Psalm 87

The city of God

God chose and loves the city of Jerusalem, as he chose and loves his people. Many of the psalms take delight in Jerusalem (Zion), the city of God: 'the city of the Great King' (Ps. 48:2). But this psalm has a wider vision. Many nations – including the Egyptians (here, Rahab) who enslaved Israel, the Babylonians who conquered them, the Philistines, and even people as far away as Tyre and Ethiopia (here, Cush) – are coming to worship the Lord in Jerusalem (vv. 4–5). The psalmist is also conscious of the privilege of being born in God's city and being recorded in God's book (v. 6).

Two big problems came with this exalted view of the city. First, the reality did not match the ideal. For much of Israel's history, Jerusalem was characterised by failed leadership, violence and fear in the streets. Religion had lost its life, spiritual power and moral authority. See for example Isaiah 1:2–9.

The second problem was complacency and presumption. The people came to regard the mere presence of the temple in the city as proof that God would protect them (Jer. 7:4). The prophets warned them against this, but the people wouldn't listen. So Jerusalem was destroyed by the Babylonians in 587 BC, and again by the Romans in AD 70. Even the Son of God was rejected and crucified when he came to his own city. No wonder Jesus wept over Jerusalem (Luke 19:41).

So when we read this exuberant psalm, we need to think beyond the stone and mortar of Jerusalem in the centuries before Christ. We look forward to the 'new Jerusalem', the centrepiece of the new heaven and new earth, which God will create when this world finally ends (Is. 65:17–25; Rev. 21:2).

REFLECTION

How are we to interpret the blessings celebrated in this psalm? The Apostle Paul can help us here. He was a deeply committed Jew by upbringing, and had the privilege of Roman citizenship. But he saw no future in either Jerusalem or Rome. His Saviour was Jesus; his 'citizenship [was] in heaven' (Phil. 3:20).

DAY 36

READ Psalm 88

Beyond blue

The psalms cover the full range of human emotion. Some take us up to heights of celebration and joy. This one takes us down to the depths.

The writer of Psalm 88 is way past just feeling depressed: 'I am overwhelmed with troubles and my life draws near to death' (v. 3). It's not simply that God has *allowed* this situation to happen. The psalmist believes that God himself has *caused* it: '*You* have put me in the lowest pit, in the darkest depths' (v. 6, my italics) ... '*You* have taken from me my closest friends and have made me repulsive to them' (v. 8). He is feeling totally alone. He thinks that God is angry with him and so has caused this misery in his life. Worst of all, he believes he is in danger of being cut off from God forever (v. 4). He also feels that God is not listening to his cries for help and has rejected him (v. 14), so concludes, 'darkness is my closest friend' (v. 18).

There is no triumphalist answer or simplistic fix to the deep depression in this psalm. Sometimes life feels like that. We are beyond well-meaning advice, happy worship songs or platitudes. But this truth remains: God does not leave us in our deepest need. So, in the midst of this dark experience, the psalmist still cries out to the 'LORD ... the God who saves me' (v. 1).

This psalm helps remind us that the Messiah suffered total aloneness. He experienced the anger of God and was cut off from God as he died on the cross. He knew that his suffering was not an accident of circumstances, but a planned action of God for our salvation (Acts 2:23).

REFLECTION

This is perhaps the saddest of all the psalms, but it gives us the words to keep praying and to keep trusting in God even when there seems to be no hope. In that sense the experience of the psalmist, the experience of Jesus who suffered and died for us, and the living power of his Spirit help all of us who have ever experienced the darkness expressed in this psalm.

The Faithful One

Love and faithfulness go together. They form the basis of all strong human relationships. They are at the core of God's character revealed in Scripture. This psalm, which is in four parts, is about the faithfulness of God:

- the first part (vv. 1–18) comprises statements *about* God and statements made *to* God, including reminders of God's covenant with King David;
- in verses 19–37, God himself is the speaker, but again the focus is on God's promises to David;
- the tone then changes (vv. 38–45) as the writer looks at the shame being suffered by one of David's kingly successors – God seems to have forgotten, or even renounced, his covenant; and
- the psalm ends (vv. 46–51) with a prayer of questioning and pleading, all on the same theme.

Throughout the psalm, the writer is looking back and remembering God's promise to David to build a dynasty for him (2 Sam. 7:11–14). The people of Israel looked for the fulfilment of this promise in the kingly line of David, but they were disappointed. Again and again the kings failed to live up to Israel's expectations. Finally, when the young king Jehoiachin was deported to Babylon (2 Kgs. 24:8, 15), it seemed like the end of the line had come and God had failed to keep his promise. This is the theme of verses 38–45. So the psalmist questions God's commitment to his promise to David (v. 49).

With the whole Bible in our hand, we see how God's promise was fulfilled in the coming of Jesus. The psalmist seems to have glimpsed this, but could not have fully understood it (Matt. 13:17). But still he begins with praise (v. 1) and ends with praise (v. 52) because he knows that God is faithful and will keep his promises.

REFLECTION

It is always easier to see God's faithfulness when we look back. Looking forward, as we face testing times, we simply have to trust him as the psalmist did (see also 1Cor. 1:8–9 and 10:13). He will not let us down.

DAY 38

READ Psalm 90

Our life is short – God is eternal

This week I learned that the fastest growing age group in the society I live in is the 100-year-plus category! Life expectancy is increasing in many developed countries. But even with the best diet, healthcare and exercise programs we will not go on indefinitely. Death is certain in the end and life passes all too quickly. That much we know.

In Psalm 90, 'A prayer of Moses', our lives are likened to a new shoot of grass, which in a hot climate is dried up and dead by evening (vv. 5–6; see also Ps. 39:4–6). Our bodies return to the dust (v. 3) and our lives 'quickly pass, and we fly away' (v. 10). But this isn't a cause for despair because the shortness and uncertainty of human life is contrasted with the everlasting nature of God. He is our eternal home (vv. 1–2).

The psalm faces up to a bigger problem than the brevity of life. We are sinful and our sinfulness provokes the anger of God (vv. 7–8). We need to be reconciled to God because facing the wrath of God without a Saviour or Mediator is a fearsome prospect (v. 11). Reflecting on our limited, uncertain and often troubled lives, he prays, 'Teach us to number our days, that we may gain a heart of wisdom' (v. 12).

This prayer for wisdom is at the heart of the psalm. This wisdom also includes understanding the love of God for sinful people like us. So he asks God to:

- have compassion on and satisfy us with his unfailing love so that we no longer need to fear either death or judgement (vv. 13–14);
- compensate our days of trouble with times of blessing (vv. 15–16); and
- show his favour on our life and daily work (v. 17).

REFLECTION

This psalm faces up to the hard realities of life, sin and death. But it also points us to the greater reality of God, who is himself our Saviour, whose love will never fail and who is our eternal home (vv. 1–2). Our relationship with him goes on beyond death, because of his gift of eternal life (John 3:16).

DAY 39

A safe place to live

God promises that 'in all things [he] works for the good of those who love him, who have been called according to his purpose' (Rom. 8:28). But notice this 'good' does not preclude the possibility of physical suffering, of 'famine or nakedness or danger or sword' (Rom. 8:35). This psalm reminds us that no harm can touch God's people unless God either allows or causes it for our ultimate good.

Taking a stand of faith (vv. 1–2)

In this opening statement of faith the psalmist uses four different titles for the Lord. He is 'the Most High', 'the Almighty', 'the LORD' (God's covenant name) and finally 'my God'. As the psalmist reflects on the character of God, no wonder he feels safe in his shelter and his shadow, under his wings (v. 1; see also Ps. 57:1). No wonder he makes God his refuge and fortress (v. 2), a safe place to live.

An appeal to trust (vv. 3–13)

He then urges others to trust God for themselves: 'If you say, "The LORD is my refuge," and you make the Most High your dwelling, no harm will overtake you' (vv. 9–10; see also Ps. 34:8). Why? Because angels will protect you (v. 11–12). Note that the devil quotes these two verses in tempting Jesus to avoid his suffering (Matt. 4:6). Note also the promised angels strengthen Jesus in his resolve to sacrifice himself for others rather than preserve his own life (Matt. 4:11; Luke 22:43).

God speaks (vv. 14–16)

The Lord highlights three aspects of his relationship with faithful believers. They love him, acknowledge his name (v. 14) and call on him in prayer (v. 15). For his part, God promises rescue and protection (v. 14) and to answer their prayers (v. 15). He also assures them of his presence in time of trouble and promises to deliver and honour them (v. 15) as well as to satisfy them with life and salvation (v. 16).

REFLECTION

This psalm speaks of living 'in the shelter of the Most High' (v. 1). The New Testament speaks of being 'in Christ'. There is no safer place to be in the face of the onslaught of the powers of sin, evil and even death.

DAY 40

Two trees

This psalm gives us one of the most attractive word pictures in all Scripture:

The righteous will flourish like a palm tree, they will grow like a cedar in Lebanon; planted in the house of the LORD, *they will flourish in the courts of our God. They will still bear fruit in old age, they will stay fresh and green, proclaiming, 'The* LORD *is upright; he is my Rock, and there is no wickedness in him' (vv. 12–15).*

It's a wonderfully encouraging picture of God's purpose for our lives. It's not a statement of what God demands from us; it's a picture of *what God will do for us.*

The psalm makes a contrast between 'senseless people', 'fools' and 'the wicked' (vv. 6–7) on the one hand, and the 'righteous' (vv. 12–15) on the other. The former spring up and die like grass (v. 7). They have no substance, no lasting purpose. But the righteous will flourish and grow (v. 12). Who are the righteous? They're those who are in right standing with God, because they rely on the mercy of God rather than on their own goodness (see Luke 18:9–24).

The righteous are going to *flourish and grow* like a tall, strong, majestic cedar of Lebanon (v. 12). The righteous will *bear fruit* like a palm tree (v. 12) – a picture of graceful natural beauty, and of a tree which provides shade and fruit – and be planted in the house of God (v. 13).

They have a deep spiritual relationship with God; their home is with the people of God; they live and grow in his presence. They have put their roots down in the Lord himself.

REFLECTION

This is God's plan and purpose for his people at whatever stage of life:

- ***flourishing and growing – being strong and bearing fruit, even in old age (v. 14; see also John 15:8);***
- ***being planted firmly in the house of God (v. 13); and***
- ***praising God and holding firm to him right through life (vv. 1–4, 14–15).***

DAY 41

READ Psalm 93

The Lord reigns

This is the first of a series of psalms (93–100) which celebrate the universal reign of God. It has the same opening line as Psalm 97: 'The LORD reigns!' How is the supremacy of God expressed? He is 'robed in majesty and armed with strength' (v. 1). It is because the Lord is in charge that the world is 'established, firm and secure' (v. 1). As the Creator, he also holds it all together. His power is seen in the 'pounding waves ... the thunder of the great waters ... the breakers of the sea' (vv. 3–4) that may leave us awestruck, but the 'LORD on high' is mightier still. He is holy (v. 5), totally separate from us because of his power, goodness and eternal nature.

As in Psalm 19, the psalmist then switches his thoughts from the supremacy of God over his creation to the law (teaching): 'Your statutes, LORD, stand firm' (v. 5). Just as the Lord holds the world together on a firm foundation (v. 1), so his Word provides the basis for his people to live by (v. 5). These links between the power of the Creator, his Word and his character are central in the Bible's revelation of Almighty God.

The Creator has spoken to humankind and set out the way for us to live. He has revealed his holy character and has provided the way for unholy people like us to get right with him – through the sacrifice of the Son of God himself.

REFLECTION

God's Kingship is revealed supremely in his Son Jesus. The world is in safe hands, and we are in safe hands, because the One on the throne is the crucified Son of God who knows what it is like to be human (Heb. 2:17–18). He who demonstrated the love and mercy of God to sinners and died for us (Rom. 5:8) is the only one worthy to hold the whole world in his hands (Rev. 5:1–10). He is a King we can love, as well as respect and honour.

DAY 42

READ Psalm 94

Evil flourishing then destroyed

Turn on the TV news and what do we see? Bombed cities, terrorist attacks and abused children. How does it make you feel? Perhaps despair at the state of the world, or maybe anger at the injustice of it all. When we react to injustice by thinking or saying, 'That's just not right' or, 'They shouldn't be allowed to get away with that', we are instinctively recognising what the Bible reveals: the created order is out of kilter when evil goes unchecked and unpunished.

Where does our sense of injustice come from? The Bible tells us that we are made in the image of God who is just: our sense of right and wrong comes from him.

This psalm celebrates God's justice. It begins with a call for God, the Judge of all the earth, to act against evil people (vv. 1–2) and then asks how long they will be allowed to get away with their wickedness (v. 3). These people:

- speak arrogantly and boast (v. 4);
- crush others and murder (vv. 5–6); and
- oppress widows, foreigners and orphans – those with no protector (v. 6).

Verses 7–11 are addressed to these evil ones: 'Does he who fashioned the ear not hear? Does he who formed the eye not see? Does he who disciplines nations not punish ... The LORD knows all human plans' (vv. 9–11). He will never forsake his people and he will bring judgement, based on righteousness, in his time (vv. 14–15). The psalmist invites others to join him in making a stand against evil (v. 16) and testifies to God's help in past difficulties (vv. 17–19).

Finally, he affirms that though 'The wicked band together against the righteous and condemn the innocent to death' (v. 21), as they did to Jesus, the Lord will destroy all evil in the end (v. 23). In the meantime, he is a fortress and refuge for his people (v. 22).

REFLECTION

In the face of the widespread injustice in our world, this psalm encourages us to make our stand, to keep praying to God to act and to remember that he will defeat and destroy evil in the end (see Matt. 13:40–43).

DAY 43

READ Psalm 95

Worshipping God

Right from the earliest days of the Christian church, this psalm has been used as a call to worship. Like many other psalms, it is itself a worship song, but it also tells us what worship involves: rejoicing, reverence for God and response to God's Word.

Rejoicing

There are times when we come into God's presence in silence, or in tears, but it is the privilege of the believer to come rejoicing (vv. 1–2). The 'shout aloud' (v. 1) is one of homage 'to the LORD' as the great King – the sort of shout or communal roar we usually reserve for rock stars or for our sporting heroes in their moments of triumph.

To 'come before him' (v. 2; literally, to come before his face) is to consciously enter into his presence. We have much to be thankful for because the God we worship is 'the Rock of our salvation' (v. 1); he is our Saviour and Deliverer. When we are joyful, we want to sing. Here we sing 'to the LORD' (v. 1) because he is 'the great God, the great King above all gods' (v. 3).

Reverence

God invites us to come into his presence rejoicing, but the key element of worship is reverence. This psalm calls us to *rejoice* because of God's greatness and to *reverence* him because of his mercy. Logically, we might want to turn this the other way round. But knowing that God is ultimately in control is a cause for joy, and we reverence him for his mercy because we dare not take that love and mercy for granted, particularly when we remember what our salvation cost the Son of God.

Response

The third element of worship is our response to the Word of God. The tone of the psalm changes abruptly (v. 8) with the warning that we should not shut our ears to what God is saying to us.

REFLECTION

Rejoicing, reverence and response: these are the essentials of worship, not just on Sundays, but each day: rejoicing in the sovereignty of God, reverencing and respecting him for his mercy and responding to his Word.

DAY 44

READ Psalm 96

A new song (1)

People sing to entertain others. If our voice is not good enough, we might sing for our own enjoyment, perhaps while driving, exercising at the gym or taking a shower. Crowds sing at football matches and in cultural celebrations. Singing in Christian worship is different, because our singing is directed to the unseen God.

This psalm, which is also found in 1 Chronicles 16, calls us to sing 'to the LORD'. It calls for a new song, a fresh song, to celebrate each day as a gift from God and to celebrate that he loves us (Lam. 3:22–23).

While the focus is on the Lord and his saving work (vv. 1–2), the psalmist also has the whole world in his sights: 'Declare his glory among the nations' (v. 3). The more we get to understand God, the more we will want to share that good news with others.

Why is God so worthy of our praise? It's because he is the great Creator, the one true living God, while 'all the gods of the nations are idols' (vv. 4–6). All humankind is called to offer worship to God 'in the splendour of his holiness' (vv. 7–9) because the Lord reigns and the whole world stands firm only because he holds it together (v. 10).

This songwriter then takes a longer view. He calls creation – the heavens and the earth; the sea, the fields and the trees – to celebrate because the Lord is coming to judge (vv. 11–13). Why is this a cause for celebration? It's because he will judge with righteousness and faithfulness (v. 13) so that the whole creation will erupt in praise (vv. 11–12). Human sinfulness has damaged the earth's environment as well as damaging people and relationships (Gen. 3:17–19). But this psalm celebrates what both Isaiah (see Is. 11) and the Apostle Paul saw was coming: a time when 'the creation itself will be liberated from its bondage to decay and brought into the freedom and glory of the children of God' (Rom. 8:21).

REFLECTION

Why not use this psalm to enlarge your thinking, inspire your worship of God and move you to praise him.

The righteous King

Like all the psalms in this group (93–100), this psalm celebrates the reign of God as King. But what sort of king is he? His power is greater than any forces in the world he made. Indeed, he controls all these forces: fire (v. 3), lightning (v. 4) and the mountains (v. 5). He is greater than any would-be 'gods' or idols that people choose to worship (vv. 7, 9), and greater than all the power of evil (v. 10). But notice the emphasis throughout this psalm on the goodness and righteousness of God:

- 'righteousness and justice are the foundation of his throne' (v. 2) – these qualities are God's qualities and characterise God's rule;
- 'the heavens proclaim his righteousness' (v. 6) – it is plain for all to see (see Ps. 19:1 and Rom. 1:20);
- his judgements are right and good – a cause for God's people to rejoice because God will sort out all injustice in his time (v. 8); and
- God's light shines on the righteous (v. 11). Who are they? All who look to God for forgiveness and mercy, who seek to follow his ways, are counted as righteous because their sin is covered by the blood sacrifice that God himself has provided (Ps. 32:1; Is. 53:5–6; Rom. 3:21–26).

Therefore the psalm ends on a note of celebration: 'Rejoice in the LORD, you who are righteous, and praise his holy name' (v. 12).

Many of the psalms express anger and perplexity at the way evil seems to flourish in our world in defiance of God. But there are many like Psalm 97 which look confidently to the day when God will sweep the world clean of evil. Strong in this conviction, the psalmist calls all faithful believers to make a stand against evil, trusting that God 'guards the lives of his faithful ones' (v. 10).

REFLECTION

The Lord's final victory is so certain that it reads in this psalm like an accomplished fact. Let that knowledge be the bedrock of our lives in this uncertain and threatening world.

DAY 46

READ Psalm 98

A new song (2)

This psalm is all joy. Like Psalm 96, it opens with the call: 'Sing to the LORD a new song'. Why? Because of God's victory. He has:

- 'done marvellous things' (v. 1);
- made his salvation and his righteousness known to the nations (v. 2); and
- 'remembered his love and his faithfulness to Israel' (v. 3).

The psalmist rejoices because God's own 'right hand and his holy arm have worked salvation' (v. 1). God himself has effectively rolled his sleeves up and acted. He has done something only God could do: defeat his enemies and save his people.

Like the psalmist, we celebrate that God himself has worked on our behalf. In his great love he has sent us his Son, the Lord Jesus Christ (John 3:16). Christ gave up his life and, in that act, saved his people and defeated his enemies: 'He himself bore our sins in his body on the cross' (1 Pet. 2:24).

The psalmist calls to 'all the earth', 'Shout for joy ... make music to the LORD' (vv. 4–5). As in Psalm 96, he invites the whole creation (vv. 7–8) to celebrate the coming of the Judge of all the earth (v. 9). The psalm expresses poetically what the Bible reveals from the beginning: that the ruin of the natural environment is inextricably linked to the sin of humankind (Gen. 3). It is only when Jesus returns at the end of time that harmony between God, his people and the creation will be restored (Rom. 8:21–23).

Again like in Psalm 96, this psalm speaks about God as Judge, one who will destroy evil and judge justly. He will not be like corrupt judges who accept bribes, or even like the best of human judges who have limited wisdom and understanding. Instead, 'He will judge the world in righteousness and the peoples with equity' (v. 9).

REFLECTION

In our worship we thank God for who he is and for what he has done for us in Christ. We also look forward to the day of his coming when his victory will be complete.

The essentials of worship

How are we to understand and properly worship God? Like Psalm 95, but in a very different way, this short psalm tells us so much about the Lord, the great King, about what he is like, about the essentials of our worship, and about how we mere mortals can approach him.

He is holy (v. 9) and just (v. 4), and communicates with us in language we understand (v. 7). We can communicate with him: he hears our prayers (v. 6). He has given us his law and makes a way of atonement when we break it (v. 7). He forgives our sin (v. 8). These timeless characteristics of God lie at the heart of true worship in every generation.

The imagery in this psalm takes us to the original tent of worship which God prescribed for the people on their journey to the Promised Land (Ex. 25:17–22). The ark (that is, container) of the covenant, which was later placed in the temple in Jerusalem, contained the tablets of the covenant law. On top of the wooden box was an 'atonement cover' or 'mercy seat' where the atoning blood of animal sacrifice was sprinkled. On top of that, at each end of the box and cast in one piece with the cover, were two cherubim, carved in gold, signifying the angelic guardians of God's holiness (see also Gen. 3:24).

So in this psalm we are to picture the King 'enthroned between the cherubim' (v. 1), where he invites worshippers to meet with him 'at his footstool' (v. 5), the mercy seat where atonement is made for sin. That was the centrepiece of Israel's worship.

REFLECTION

How are we to understand and relate to the imagery in this psalm? We are not 'under the law' (Rom. 6:14), but the law still reveals God's holy character and that has not changed. We no longer need an ark or mercy seat because God himself, in the person of his Son Jesus, has provided the sacrifice for our sin, once for all and for ever (Heb. 7: 23–27). And we have the privilege of approaching the throne of God with boldness (Heb. 4:14–16) because we have access through faith in Jesus Christ (Rom. 5:1–2).

DAY 48

READ Psalm 100

Belonging to God's people

So much truth is packed into this short, exuberant song of praise about:

- God: he is good, and full of mercy and truth;
- believers: we are his people, the sheep of his pasture; and
- his invitation to us: to praise him, serve him, come to him, know that he is God and be thankful.

The psalm is not addressed to God. Rather it calls us to join in worshipping him. Like Psalm 98, it's full of joyful celebration. We are encouraged to 'Shout for joy', and to express that joy with singing (v. 1). We are reassured that 'the LORD is God' and there is no other (v. 3). He made us, but the focus here is not so much on our creation as the fact that he made us 'his people' (v. 3) by calling us to faith. We belong to him, like sheep belong to the Good Shepherd. A personal relationship with God through faith in Jesus Christ is very precious, but this psalm celebrates the truth that if we belong to God, then we also belong to his people.

This psalm was written in the days of the temple, when worshippers would enter through its gates and into its courts to praise God (v. 4). We don't need a physical building to enter the presence of God. We come through faith in Jesus Christ, our Lord and Saviour, who has opened up the way to God for us (Rom. 5:1–2; Heb. 10:19–23). Like the psalmist, we have great reason to be thankful because 'the LORD is good' (v. 5). His love will never end and he will remain faithful to all generations of his people, all around the world, to the end of time.

REFLECTION

Belonging to God's people is one of the great blessings highlighted in the psalms and indeed throughout the Bible: belonging not just to an earthly family or a local tribe, but also to a global family of believers drawn from 'every nation, tribe, people and language' (Rev. 7:9).

REFERENCES

1 A longer devotion looking at this psalm first appeared in my book *A Better Way to Live* (Acorn Press, 2016).

2 This possibly refers to the defeat of the ten tribes of Israel by the Assyrian superpower in 722 BC.

MORE IN THIS SERIES

ROMANS
Momentous News
By David Cook
ISBN: 978-1-906173-24-1

MARK
The Suffering Servant
By Jeremy McQuoid
ISBN: 978-1-906173-55-5

DANIEL
Far From Home
By Justin Mote
ISBN: 978-1-906173-68-5

1 THESSALONIANS
Living for Jesus
By Julia Marsden
ISBN: 978-1-906173-67-8

PHILIPPIANS
Press Towards the Goal
By Kay Mumford
ISBN: 978-1-909611-31-3

GALATIANS
The Life I Now Live
By Peter Mead
ISBN: 978-1-910587-09-6

ACTS
To the Ends of the Earth
By David Cook
ISBN: 978-1-909611-02-3

EZEKIEL
For His Glory
By Peter Lau
ISBN: 978-1-909611-83-2

JOHN
Never Thirst Again
By David Cook
ISBN: 978-1-909611-30-6

and more at... 

To place an order call: **0330 2233 423** email: **sales@10ofthose.com**
or order online: **www.10ofthose.com**

Graham Hooper
PSALMS
SONGS FROM THE HEART
VOLUME 2
48 UNDATED DEVOTIONS THROUGH PSALMS 51–100

10 Publishing
a division of 10 of those.com